Never Lose A Trade Again

Author | Tamer Abbas

Content

Introduction

My name is Tamer Abbas, born and lived in Cairo, Egypt.

Since my graduation as an accountant, from faculty of commerce - Ain Shams University in year 1995 and I'm trying to find myself by applying for jobs that does not fit my character so I've been a disk jockey in bars, hotels for almost 3 years and at the same time an accountant for almost two years and half in Egypt Air. One day I took an honest moment with myself and looked to my future with a scary eyes " Is this the life that I want to live", disk jockey in the night and in the morning an employee?!!. No this is not my dream and my destiny, all of a sudden I made a turning point decision to quit both jobs and traveled to New York searching for my chances of better future, at this time all people around me called me crazy, since it was not about money, my salary as DJ was quite good, fancy life in the night, reputable company to be part of in the morning.

Back to New York, after applying for different jobs including a delivery boy in Domino's Pizza, man-day in shoe shop etc… for 8 months, I discovered that my future also not in New York, but I was waiting for any chance to tell myself that I was wrong, during this period, me and my young brother "Ahmed" who was living in New Jersey for almost 4 years met several times during the holidays.

By this time "Ashraf" my best friend was covering the 1998 FIFA World Cup in France and he contacted me over the phone telling me that there is a good chance for me to be hired in the Egyptian Radio & TV Union - since they were establishing " Nile Thematic Channels", and the board was looking for newly graduated, so I took my chances and told myself - New York will be there if things did not went well, I left my things and went to

Cairo once again, It took 1 long month before attending the interview, during this month I kept telling myself that I have to go back to New York, anyway I made the interview and took the job as a TV production assistant under training, things was fine but I was not happy, month after month, I promised myself to be good in the job even if it was not my dream, until I find another way.

After 4 years, I was a reputable Production Manager and have a lot of good friends & connections, made a lot of projects for Film & TV and decided to open my own company "Egypt Productions" for film & TV production.

In 2004, I took the risk and invest all the money that I have in the company and started to promote the company.

While doing so, my young brother "Ahmed" mentioned trading stocks on Wall Street over the phone, he was talking about his experience, but while waiting for projects to come I did asked him on how to apply for foreigner account with a broker from USA, he did recommend me Ameritrade, I googled, made some researches then applied for a foreign margin account, 15 days later I did wired the first $2,000 to fund my account, then started to trade like a fool who was fascinated by the stock market and its daily huge gains for some individual stocks, without any experience or plan, without knowing why I'm losing that big or winning that small rarely, until my account dried in less than a month.

Give it another try for the second time and wired another $2000, and kept trading with the same way.

By the time I lost hope of being good in trading, while Film & TV projects start to come to the company, start to focus on my work and left that passion behind me.

From 2004 through 2008, things went well, got married in 2005, first baby girl "Mira" in late 2006, the business was quite good and my life went from good to better until the financial crises in 2008, most of the foreign film & TV projects canceled and the overall future look was not good.

In year 2009, my big brother "Wael" recommend to invest in Egyptian Stock Exchange since there was a limit to gain or loss per day, i.e. 5% maximum gain then the stock will be stopped from trading. I did follow since I have no other option and invest in Egyptian Stock Exchange more than EGP150,000 at this time which were equal around $30,000, "Wael" my big brother recommends some stocks with a very solid financial to buy and I did, but at the wrong time because I did not have any idea about technical indicators.

By the following month I lost almost half of the money, and It became a challenge to me, to know why I'm losing, and if the companies in that good financial, why its price per share drops that way.

I was seeking an answer from people around, then reading without any progress.

I start to think of a way, to measure my trades by not buying any stock unless its volume rise by at least 5% of its outstanding shares, but also did not work well.

In late 2009, I had a Film Project, so I did stop trading after losing more than 70% of the fund and when I did finish my project, I decided to raise funds to my account to reach almost EGP 650,000 or almost $130,000, and start to trade again, until I lost more than EGP500,000, or almost $100,000 by the end of year 2010.

By this time, my only passion was trading, I kept telling myself that their was nothing wrong with me but the Egyptian market is manipulated, one of my friends told me, try to study charts, I said if you have the money to control any stock, then the chart will follow, it is financial matter not a technical at all.

At the beginning of 2010, I changed the market but not the dream, I went back to Wall Street and fund my account with the rest of the money that I had, then started to look for the volume when trading, then bit by bit while reading I discovered that no matter how the company's financial is healthy, they all under pressure.

So I changed my way in trading and picked stocks that have a good news, so I played news only.

It did work for me sometimes but not all the time, and I noticed that even when the company had a good news, yet the price did not react the way it should, in some cases, after a moderate surge in price, by the end of the day the price were closing in the red territory, so I said to myself, It is not about volume or news or fundamental, something else have a greater effect, especially while monitoring other stocks that made more than 20% gains in one day without any public news.

The revolution in Egypt started in early 2011, my Film and TV business stopped completely, I had a rough time finding a solution just like everybody else, and decided to learn more about the art of trading.

Not only this, while everybody around was pushing me, to let my passion go and find a job since I was having a moderate reputation in the film and TV business, I kept my brain to think in one track, trading is my future, and it should be.

So, I started to search for good technical indicators, from here I did start to monitor, exam more and trade less, I did start to trade from charts and applied more than 150 indicators/study to my charts, two or 3, even 5 at a time. Switch them, adjust them, throw them away and get new ones, read more than 100 books, then reading books for people whom made success through world competitions in recent years like Larry Williams, Chuck Hughes, applying authors' ideas, improving my trades.

Until one day, I was able to see which technique is working well for me, use the right study and the right indicator, I was able to read any stock chart in one deep look, in less than a minute I can tell you where it will go, is it good for trading or there will be a counter selling.

I was able to see the market pretty much naked.

This book is a straightforward one, it is organized to show step by step how to build your trading plan, how to build your trading chart from scratch, reach your financial freedom in less time, this is my experience so far and still learning, enjoy.

Trading ... Our Interest!!!

Any tradable market goes through cycles, ups..downs..sideways.

Trading at itself can be a heart attack if you do not know what and when to trade.

Some cycles takes more than other cycles, once a stock in the move, it will continue to move either up or down until it forced to ease, accumulate then change the direction of its trend, it do so by a forcing power, a group or someone who care to change the present cycle, this one might be an insider who knows something, market maker or any investor.

It is not our interest in this book to dig to know who is behind this, our interest is;

• To select the right stocks to trade by ranking them according to their volatility, on other words, which one of them offers better wild price swings thus potential return vs. risk and time.

• To be able to clearly identify the fake breakout to ignore, and the true one to ride in early stage.

- To sit tight and let our profits run with confidence, until the end of the trend. This might take hours, days or even weeks.

- That being identified, our focus will be on price action and some technical indicators.

- The most important thing is to trade with discipline and with a position-sizing plan.

- Now, let's take off our shoes by leaving our (ready-to-use) thoughts outside and go through this book to see the Stock Market naked.

Range Bar Charts. One chart tells everything

To start, let me give you a brief history on range bars. In 1995 a Brazilian broker and trader named Vicente M. Nicolellis Jr. decided he needed a better approach to handle the volatility of his local markets in Sao Paulo where he operated his trading desk.

His solution was to eliminate the time element from the equation and instead just concentrate on the price action.

To do this he developed an extremely promising approach called constant range bars, which had a number of characteristics:

- Each bar is the same height because the range is constant

- The close of the bar has been always at the high or low of the bar

- The openness of a bar is always one tick above or below the preceding bar

- The time period covered by each bar is variable as time is irrelevant to range bar creation

Using this method a trader could choose the range they found most useful in their methods and apply new approaches those were otherwise unavailable using their previous charts.

This new range bar development provided Mr. Nicolellis many advantages over time-based charting.

For one, using range bars helps smooth out the price action and eliminates a lot of the market noise.

Since only price matters to range bar creation and not time, periods of chopping action are minimized and false signals are reduced.

We can see in the charts below how effective this can be, where extra bars print in, the strong trending move up (allowing us additional entry opportunities) while less bars print, while price is moving slowly and is quite choppy (thus keeping us out of false moves).

Using range bars also more clearly highlights potential areas of support and resistance.

But probably the most important advantage of range bar charts is that they allow us to minimize or in some cases even eliminate the lag time of indicators.

Using indicators may only be a small part of a comprehensive overall trading approach, but they can still be highly effective if used in a way that minimizes the noise and false signals.

By focusing on price alone and removing the time element, many indicators become much more accurate and powerful.

For example, in The Elite Range Bar System we use moving averages to help us time our trades by taking entries in line with short and medium-term momentum.

By removing time we are able to focus on the movement of price itself that allows us to be more precise.

Where a trader might normally have to wait for a bar to close, we can enter within that bar by trading strictly off the movement and momentum of price.

This makes for an extremely effective trading approach!

Let's see some examples of Range Bar Charts Vs. Time-based charts for the same daily - one-year period.

SPX: Daily 1 Year - Range Bar Chart

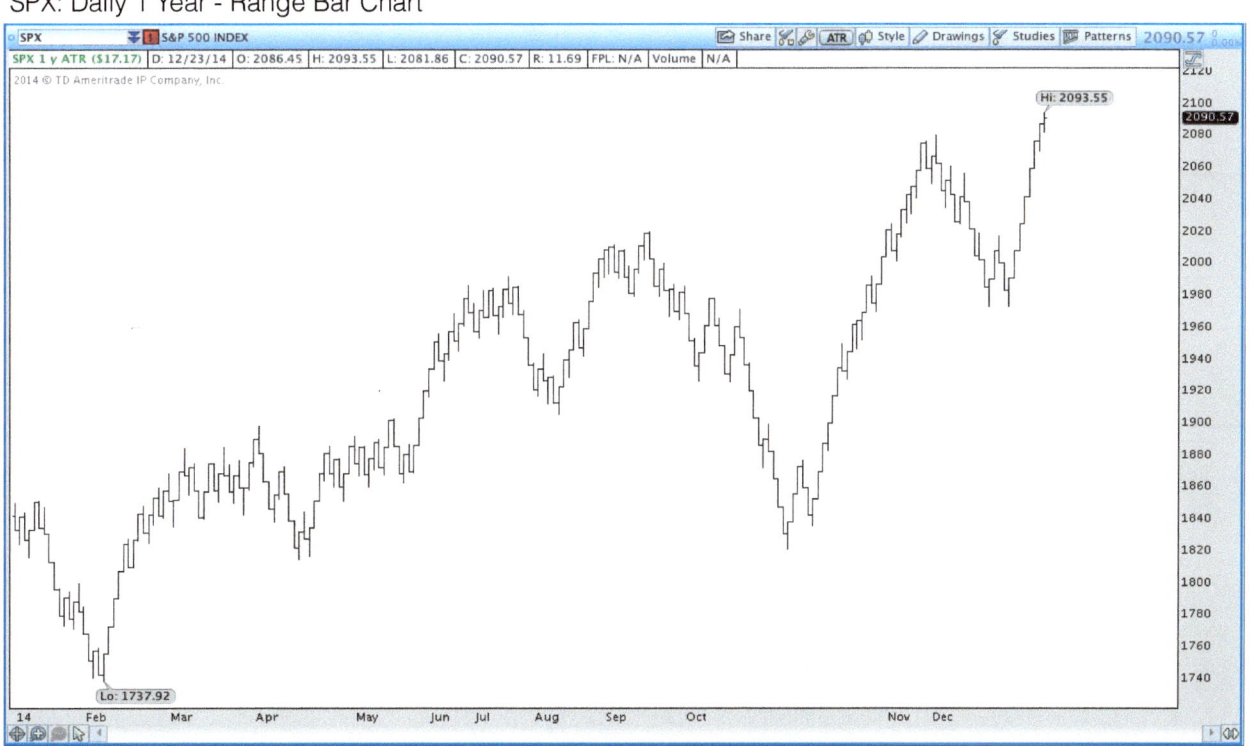

SPX: Daily 1 Year - Time Based Chart

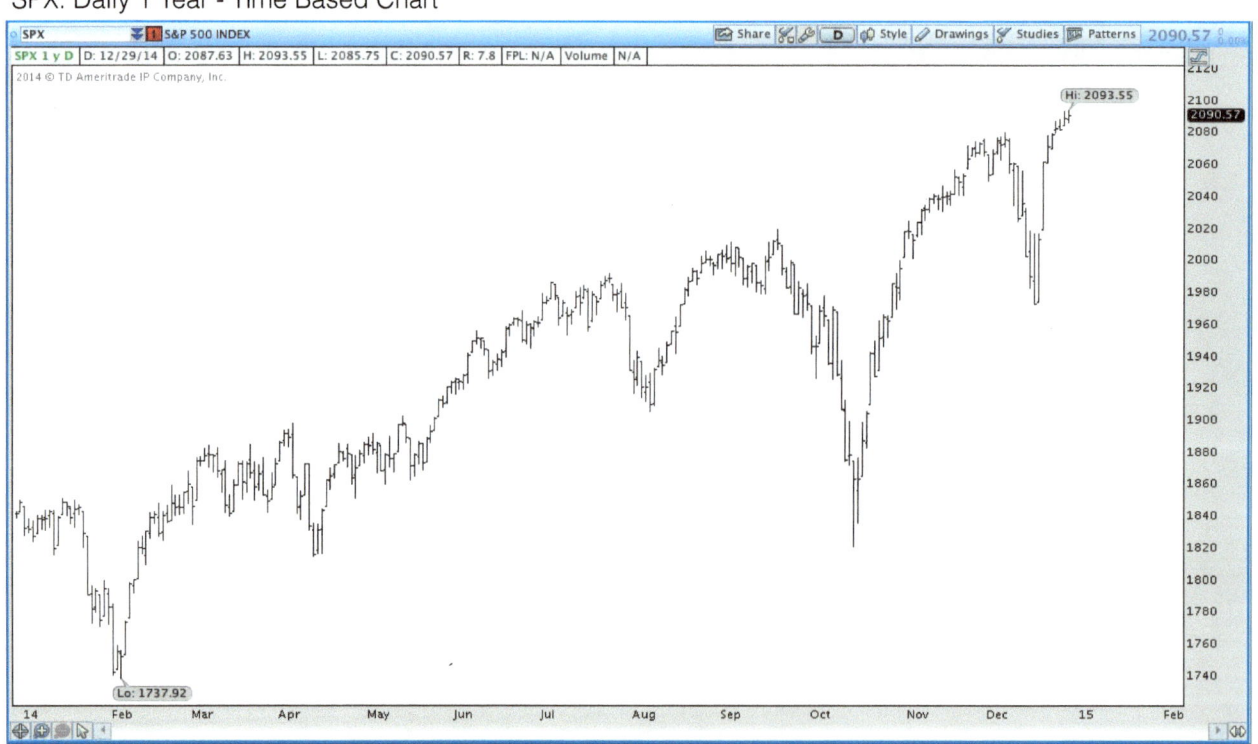

JOB: Daily 1 Year - Range Bar Chart

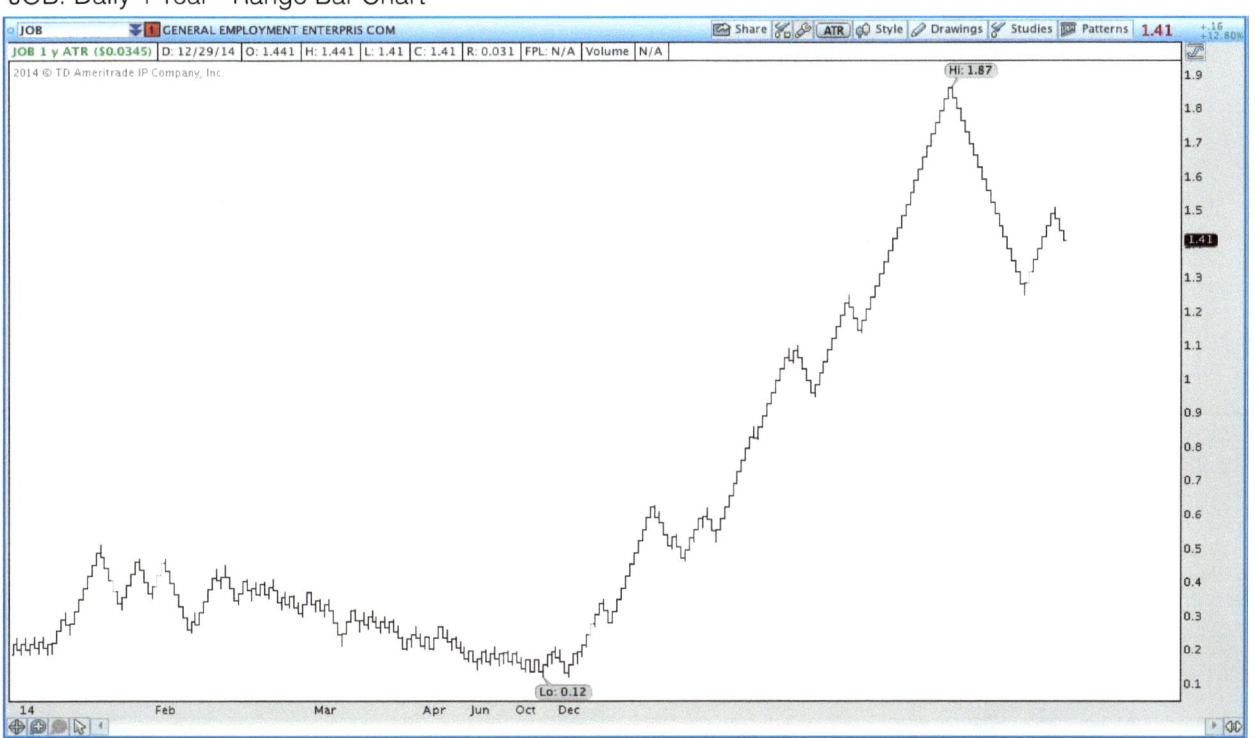

JOB: Daily 1 Year - Time Based Chart

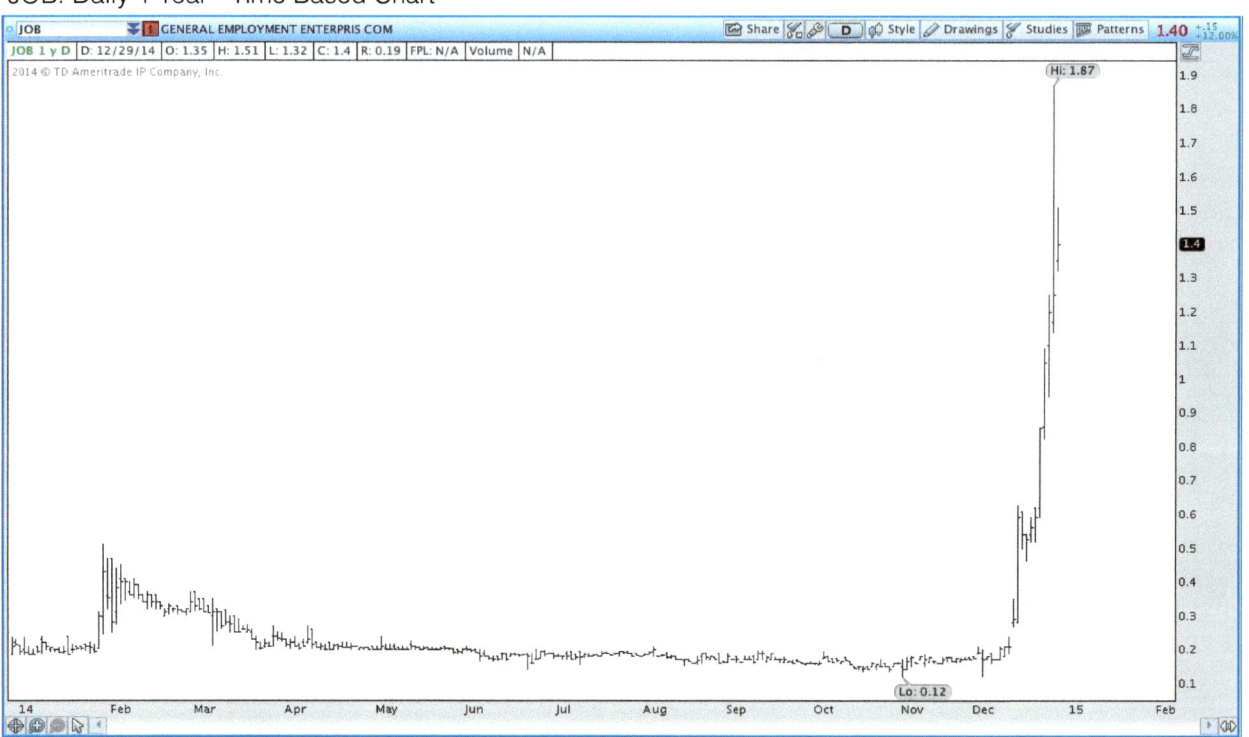

LIVE: Daily 1 Year - Range Bar Chart

LIVE: Daily 1 Year - Time Based Chart

The Beauty of ATR% "Average True Range Percentage"

You do not want to spend one year investing your money in an equity with very solid fundamental and good technical but only offers a return between 5% - 10% through this year, while watching every day equities that offers a return of 10% - 50% in one day or a week, especially when you are swing or short term trader.

So we need to find a way to measure and rank all stocks according to what they can offer as a return.

One more important advantage while using Range Bar charts that you can adjust its range bars to represent the "average true range" of any stock.

DEFINITION OF 'AVERAGE TRUE RANGE - ATR'

A measure of volatility introduced by Welles Wilder in his book: New Concepts in Technical Trading Systems.

The true range indicator is the greatest of the following:

• Current high less the current low.

• The absolute value of the current high less the previous close.

• The absolute value of the current low less the previous close.

The average true range is a moving average (generally 14-days) of the true ranges.

While it is a good method to use, But the absolute ATR dollar value says little in terms of ranking stocks.

While searching for quality stocks that offers wild price swings, one of the best methods is ATR%

ATR Percent = (ATR(14)/last)*100

By applying the factor of a percentage of the ATR to the recent close – stocks with a higher percentage will be more volatile than those with lower percentages.

Now let's compare and rank stocks based on their ATR% to see if it can tell more.

For example; in the next three charts we have SPX, JOB and LIVE stocks, when three of them trending, and you want to buy long one of them, which one is better for you to buy!!?. You need to know which one of them is offering better return vs. risk & time.

SPX 1 year ATR is ($17.17), and last price is $2090.57, that means $17.17/$2090.57 = ATR%0.82.

JOB 1year ATR is ($0.0345), and last price is $1.42, that means $0.03/$1.4 = ATR%2.43.

And LIVE 1year ATR is ($0.50), and last price is $3.95, that means $0.50/$3.95 = ATR%12.65.

Now we know that while JOB is cheaper than SPX, but it is offering much better price swings.

From the other hand, while JOB is cheaper than LIVE, yet LIVE is ranked higher in volatility than JOB and can perform better in less time.

Now we can focus on what LIVE is offering, when and only when it does make a true breakout and start to trend.

SPX 1 Year ATR ($17.17) - ATR% (0.82) - Range Bar Chart

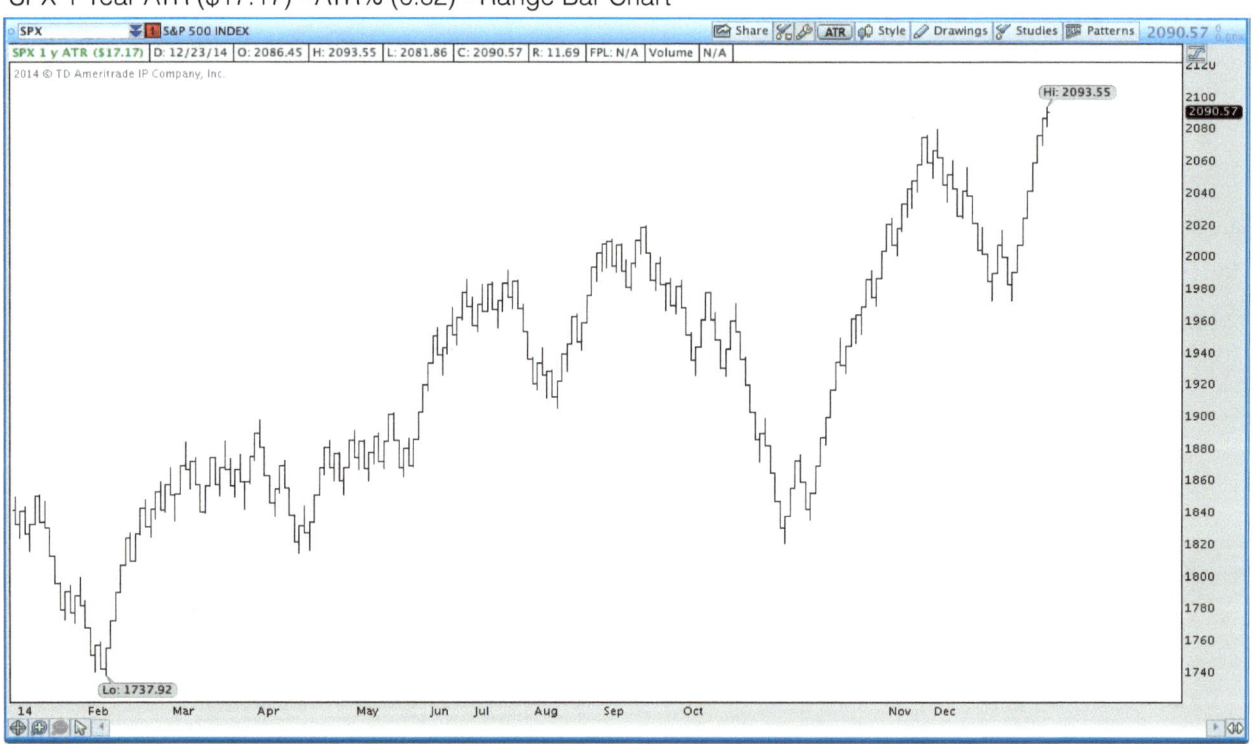

JOB 1 Year ATR ($0.0345) - ATR% (2.43) - Range Bar Chart

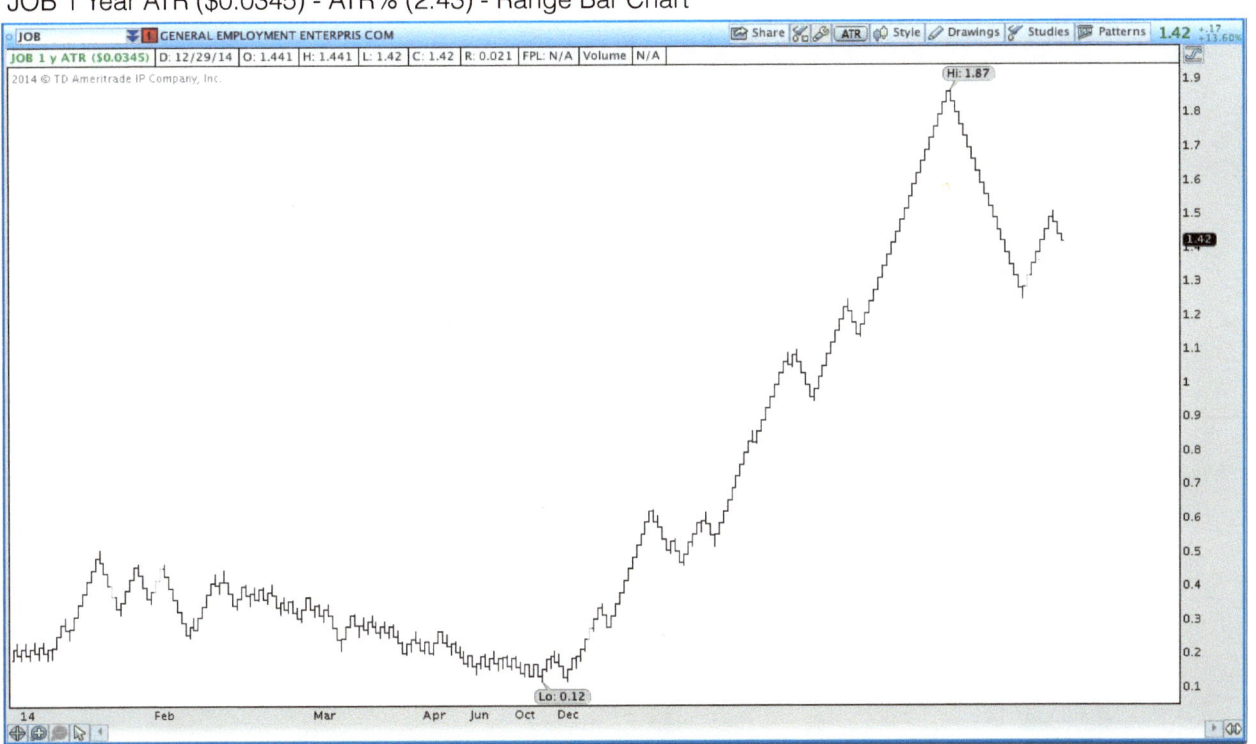

LIVE 1 Year ATR ($0.50) - ATR% (12.65) - Range Bar Chart

Ichimoku Clouds ... what an Indicator!!?

Do you remember when we said earlier "sit tight with confidence", Ichimoku helps you doing so. It tells you if the next range bar either up or down will be safe for your open position to wait for without panic, or you should wrap and close your position.

The cloud lines simply tell you ahead part of the very near future.

Ichimoku Clouds, also known as Ichimoku Kinko Hyo, is a versatile indicator that defines support and resistance, identifies trend direction, gauges momentum and provides trading signals.

Ichimoku Kinko Hyo translates into "one look equilibrium chart". With one look, chartists can identify the trend and look for potential signals within that trend. The indicator was developed by Goichi Hosoda, a journalist, and published in his 1969 book.

Calculation

Four of the five plots within the Ichimoku Cloud are based on the average of the high and low over a given period of time. For example, the first plot is simply an average of the 9-day high and 9-day low.

Tenkan-sen (Conversion Line): (9-period high + 9-period low)/2))

The default setting is 9 periods and can be adjusted. On a Range Bar chart, this line is the mid point of the 9 Bars high-low range.

Kijun-sen (Base Line): (26-period high + 26-period low)/2))

The default setting is 26 periods and can be adjusted. On a Range Bar chart, this line is the mid point of the 26 Bars high-low range.

Senkou Span A (Leading Span A): (Conversion Line + Base Line)/2))

This is the midpoint between the Conversion Line and the Base Line.

The Leading Span A forms one of the two Cloud boundaries. It is referred to as "Leading" because it is plotted 26 periods in the future and forms the faster Cloud boundary.

Senkou Span B (Leading Span B): (52-period high + 52-period low)/2))

On the Range Bar chart, this line is the mid point of the 52 Bars high-low range.

The default calculation setting is 52 periods, but can be adjusted. This value is plotted 26 periods in the future and forms the slower Cloud boundary.

Chikou Span (Lagging Span): Close plotted 26 Bars in the past

The default setting is 26 periods, but can be adjusted.

In this book we will use Ichimoku clouds with a little tweak on its standards to help us achieve our main strategy, which is trading strong trends only.

To do so, from ichimoku setup, we will hide Tenkan-sen, Kijun-sen and Chikou Span (Lagging Span)

And use only Senkou Span A (Leading Span A) and Senkou Span B (Leading Span B)

As you can see in the next charts, to identify the overall trend using the Clouds, the up-trend is strengthened when the Leading Span A (blue cloud line) is rising and above the Leading Span B (red cloud line). This situation produces a yellow Cloud. Conversely, a down-trend is reinforced when the Leading Span A (blue cloud line) is falling and below the Leading Span B (red cloud line). This situation produces a red Cloud.

Because the Cloud is shifted forward 26 days, it also provides a glimpse of future support or resistance.

Now let's see the next charts.

SPX 1 Year ATR ($17.17) - ATR% (0.82) - Range Bar Chart

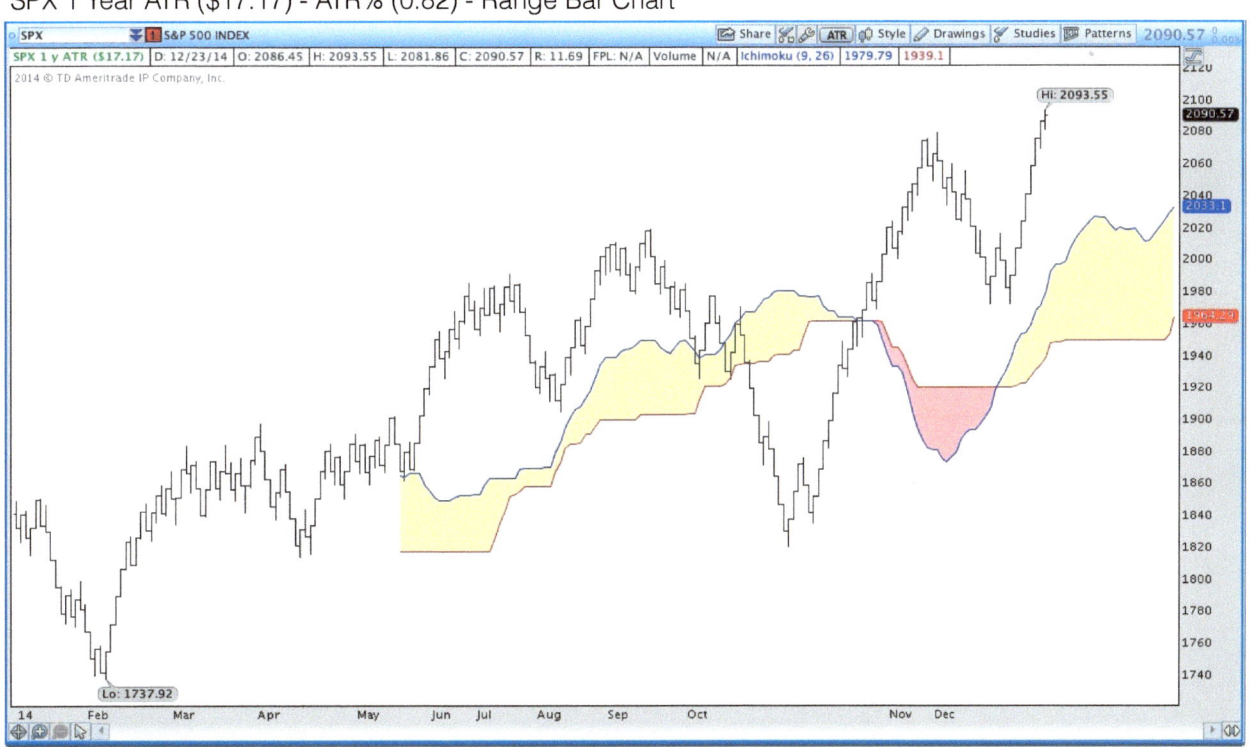

The previous (SPX chart) shows two things, that it is a major up-trend that starts from point1902 to 2093.55 within the period of 10/20/2014 to 12/23/2014, gaining more than 109% in almost 2 months.

From the Ichimoku clouds, we can see that while we did not catch the first wave of the major trend or its retrace from the beginning, but still we have a room for entry and catch the second wave.

Kindly to remember the ATR% volatility valuation and the return offered by SPX vs. risk & time compared with next chart of JOB, since both of them on major up trend.

JOB 1 Year ATR ($0.0345) - ATR% (2.43) - Range Bar Chart

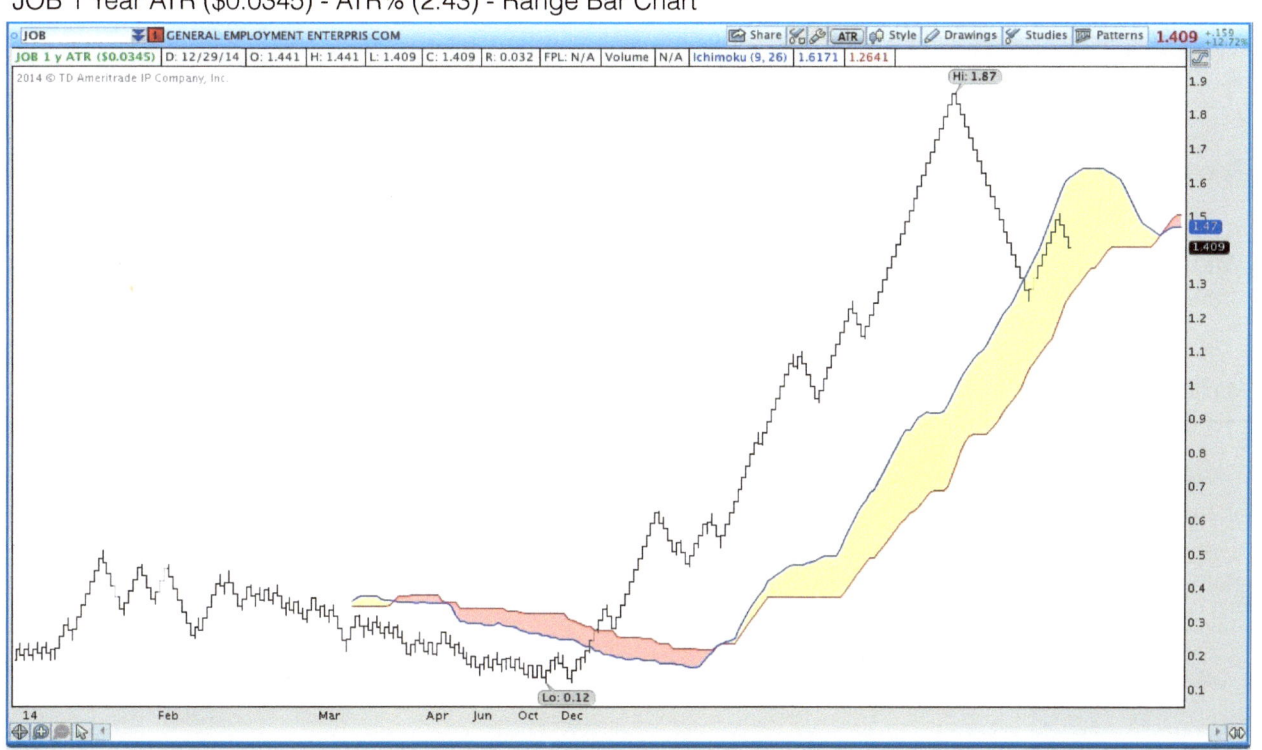

The previous (JOB chart) shows a lot, it tells that the major up trend starts from point 0.28 all the way up to 1.87 from 12/15/2014 : 26/12/2014 gaining more than 667% in only 9 days.

Previous SPX chart offered 119% on return over a longer time period of almost 2 months.

We know from chapter 3 (The Beauty of ATR%) that JOB volatility percentage offers better wild price swings than SPX volatility percentage.

While we have a minor retracement in the up trend, but because of "Ichimoku Clouds" we can now sit tight without panic all the way up to at least 1.5 with confidence.

Also it tells us one important thing when looking at the end of the "Ichimoku Clouds" that this major trend is eased, and an accumulation or down-trend is reinforced when the Leading Span A (blue cloud line) falls below the Leading Span B (red cloud line) and produced a red Cloud.

This situation means that it is time for long positions to be closed and Short positions may opens.

LIVE 1 Year ATR ($0.50) - ATR% (12.65) - Range Bar Chart

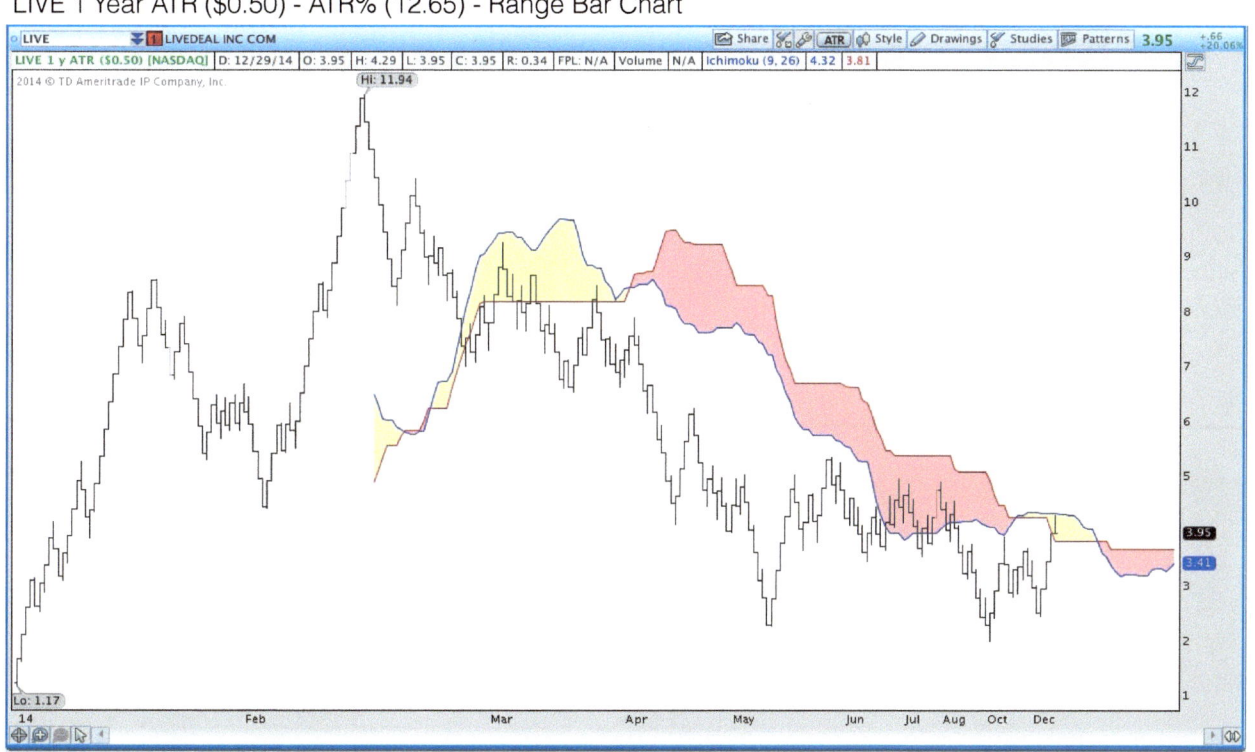

35

The previous (LIVE chart) shows that we have to wait until the Leading Span A (blue cloud line) is rising and above the Leading Span B (red cloud line) and the yellow Cloud is produced to enter an open long position

Also LIVE still in accumulation and true breakout not yet to be recognized.

At the end, applying "Ichimoku Clouds" to our range bar charts giving us confidence in trading trends but still not enough.

Now we are on the right track, let's enhance our range bar chart and move to the next level.

"HighestHigh - LowestLow" - A good start

Any tradable market produces a lot of whipsaws simply to accumulate while to unfold weak hands or make false/fake breakouts to distribute while going throw down-trend.

While enhancing our chart ability to produce true signals, one of the most powerful studies that avoids us most of this whipsaws and false/fake breakouts is Highest High/Lowest Low (HH/LL), and it is more powerful and reliable while using Range Bar Charts, and here is why.

The study plots the highest high and the lowest low for the number of periods you specify.

Parameters:
Some prefer to use 10 periods or 20 periods, in our book we will use.
- HighestHigh Period (14) - the number of bars, or interval, used to determine the highest high.
- LowestLow Period (14) - the number of bars, or interval, used to determine the lowest low.

Computation
The mathematics defines an envelope of values by using the highest high and lowest low over a duration of n prior periods.

The rules generally followed for this study are:
- Enter the market when one of the bands is penetrated. This indicates a possible start of a trend.
- Exit and reverse the position when the opposite band is penetrated.

All the whipsaws and false/fake breakouts done within tight ranges using different small periods of moving averages, but it will not break up the highest high band because when it do so, a lot of major players will be interested, the same goes on the lowest low if breaks down, a lot of major players will consider unfold their hands thus making a major move and volume either up or down that the market maker or the insiders do not want to happen at this time.

When using this study on a daily time-based charts it means that the study will count only prior 14 bars/days.

While using Range Bar Charts will count the last 14 printed bars which might count more than 50 bars/days on the time-based chart.

So when we apply HH/LL on Range Bar Charts, it is even stronger, effective and most of the time produce true breakout or breakdown.

Let's exam the next charts, and find what it can tell.

SPX 1 Year ATR ($17.17) - ATR% (0.82) - Range Bar Chart

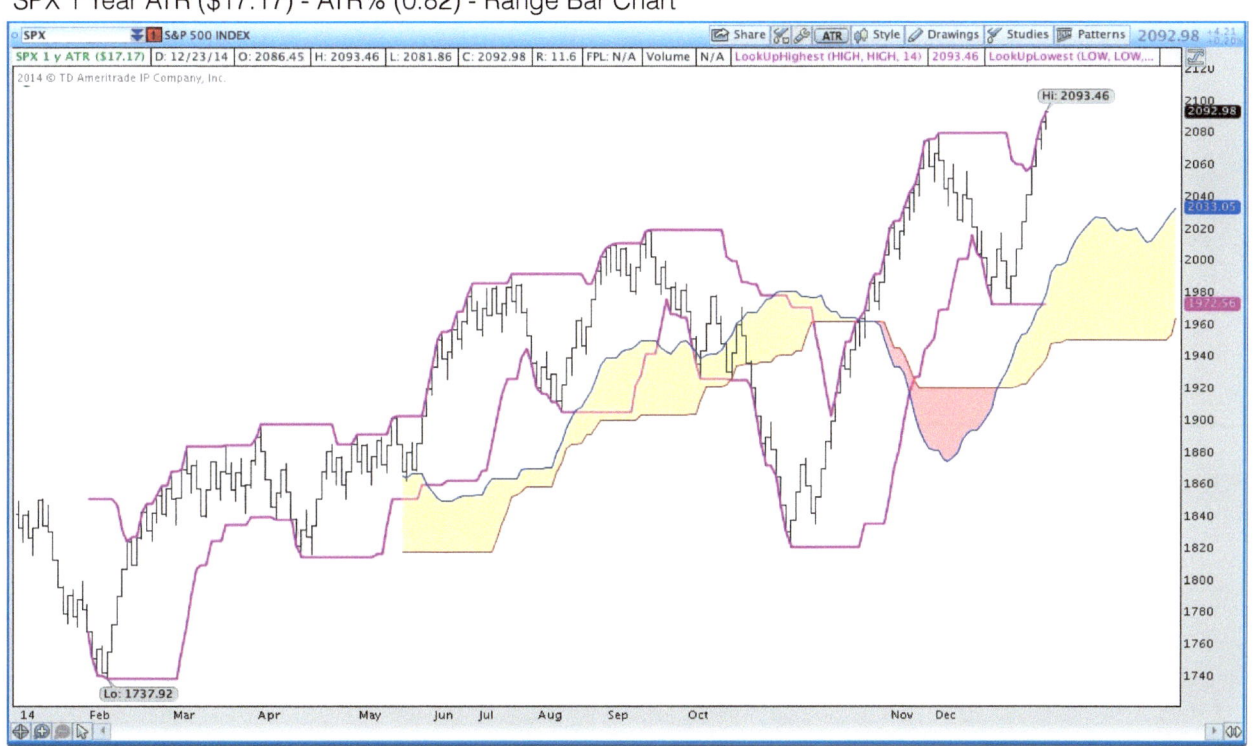

The previous (SPX chart) show that we would open a long position when the price hit 1903 points, and ride a major trend all the way up to 2080 points, our stop loss would be around 2018 points as we use our stop loss right behind the lowest low boarder.

Also with confidence generated from Ichimoku, we know that this decline in price that happens in the beginning of December was only a retrace but we still in the main major up-trend, so it is better to exit and lock our profits at the point 2018 and reopen the long position once again when the price hit the point 2060 to continue the major up-trend.

This way we save our backs from any counter selling that might occur.

JOB 1 Year ATR ($0.0345) - ATR% (2.43) - Range Bar Chart

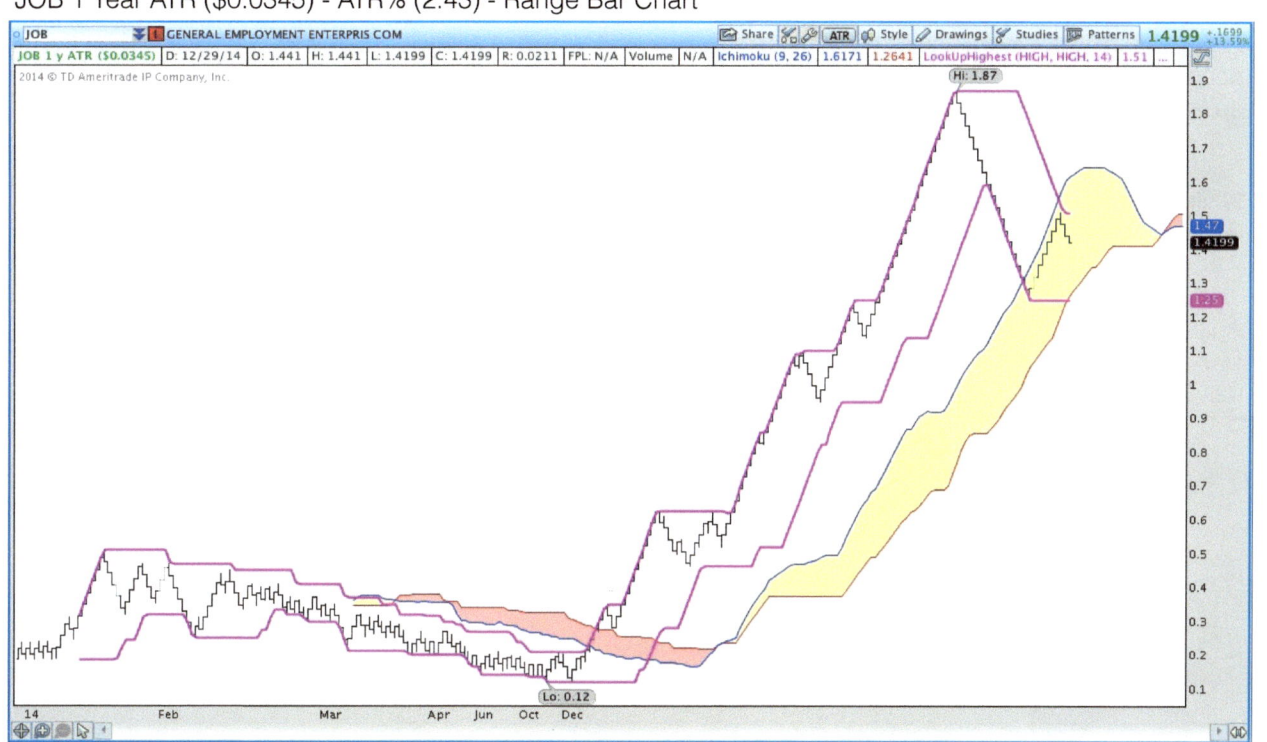

The previous (Job chart) shows a beautiful one, straight forward, we would open a long position when the price hit 0.21 but because Ichimoku indicator shows that we were having a resistance cloud between 0.22 up to 0.27, so it is wiser to open our long position when the price hit 0.27.

While price action did make 3 or 4 minor retrace, but the up trend kept healthy and did not break down the lowest low boarder at any time all the way up to 1.58 or so.

Again with confidence that produced by Ichimoku, we would ride the up-trend all the way up and raise our stop loss behind the LowestLow line, and we were able to lock most of our profits and sell when the up-trend were confirmed to be eased.

LIVE 1 Year ATR ($0.50) - ATR% (12.65) - Range Bar Chart

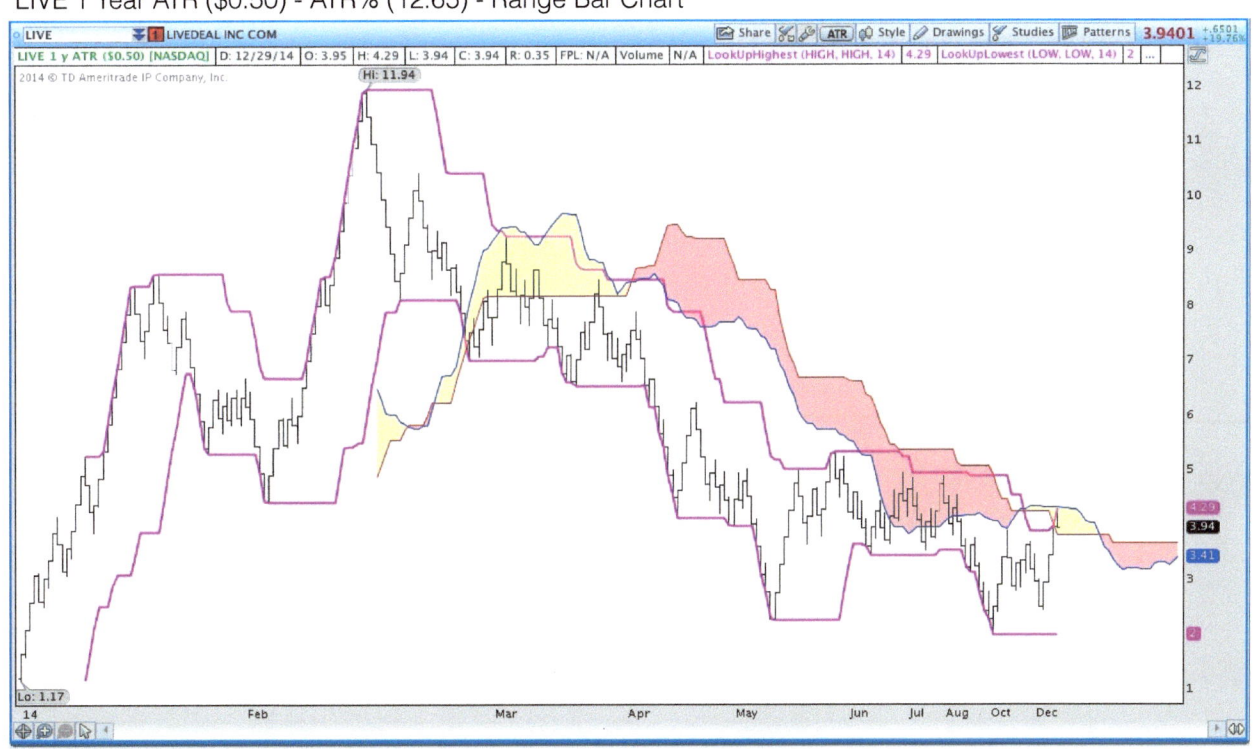

The previous (LIVE chart) shows that it did signal a breakout and that the train is about to leave the station in a day or two, we just need to wait for a confirmation ticket from Ichimoku because the price should be over the cloud and the line of span A (blue line) did not cross the line of span B (red line) and opened a yellow cloud yet.

This chart teaches us that waiting with our money outside is better than to jump-in early and suffering badly.

Another fact that there is no one study or indicator can stand alone, and that we need more than one confirmation to rely on.

Because we are not isolated from the world, there is a must to see what crowd looking at, in the next chapter, we will see Moving Averages and how we can benefit from it to enhance our chart.

Moving Average Two Lines Exceptional, is what crowd looking at, and so you

All the back-test studies that came under my eyes while searching for best indicator to use, said loud and clear that any kind of moving averages applied (Simple, Weighted, Hull and Exceptional) produced a lot of whipsaws and false signals.

Also the results of applying moving averages as an indicator that produce entry/exit signals, did not approach by any how the 55% success on any backtest regardless the length of it, and the most succeeded on was MA Exceptional.

But why we have that interest in applying this indicator in our chart!!?.

Using moving average two lines is to see what the crowd looking at, and to make sure that we are on the right track.

And since most of the key players trading the golden/death cross to make their moves, so when we are looking at MA two lines Exceptional, we are looking forward to see huge volume that will support the trend run. But the actual truth breaks happened before the cross itself because it is lagging indicator.

However, using MA two lines Exceptional with Range Bar Chart minimize its lagging and produce better signals than applying it to time-based chart.

To understand a Golden/Death cross, first you have to get to grips with the idea of moving averages.

A moving average takes the closing price of a stock from each of the previous days over a given period (say 50 days/bars) and then divides it by the same number (50) to arrive at an average.

As each day/Range Bar passes the entire data set is updated, which is what makes this a 'moving' average.

Investors like this calculation because it strips out the intra-day volatility of a share price ("noise") to give a fixed trend that can be tracked over a given time frame.

On a stock chart, the golden cross occurs when the 50-day MA rises sharply and crosses over the 200-day MA. This is seen as bullish.

According to Joseph Granville, a famous technician from the 1960's (who set out 8 famous rules for trading the 200-day MA), a golden cross can only occur when **both** the 50-day and 200-day moving averages are rising.

Others take a less stringent view on this.

Usually, a golden cross is associated with sharp upward price movement and can be used as a buy signal in the belief that a significant up-trend will follow.

The reverse of this event is known as a Death Cross where the 50-day MA falls below the 200-day MA, a bearish signal.

A related theory is the idea that, if the 50-day MA is **much** higher than the 200-day MA (which happens with a fast run up in price), the stock is likely to be temporarily overbought (therefore, overvalued) which is bearish for the short-run.

Let's study the next charts.

SPX 1 Year ATR ($17.17) - ATR% (0.82) - Range Bar Chart

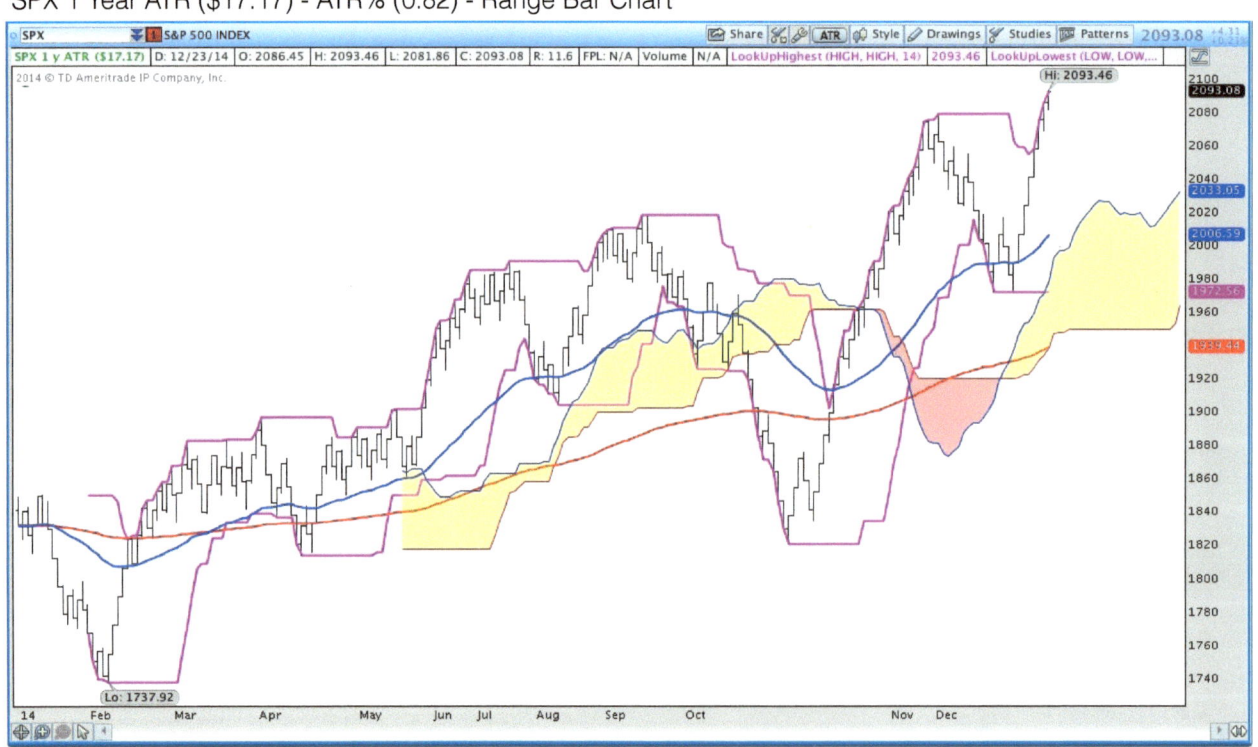

The previous (SPX chart) set the end of the conversation and prove our saying, if we did count on MA two lines Exceptional to produce buying and selling signals, we were forced to sell our stocks if we did buy it with margin when prices declined from $2020 to $1820 from mid September to mid October, and lost all our profits that were made from March through October.

While Ichimoku Clouds and HH/LL warned loudly that there is a decline coming and we should close our long positions when the price hits $1980.

Even in early March when the golden cross happens, the price didn't trend that much and shortly after it did declined once again in mid April.

JOB 1 Year ATR ($0.0345) - ATR% (2.43) - Range Bar Chart

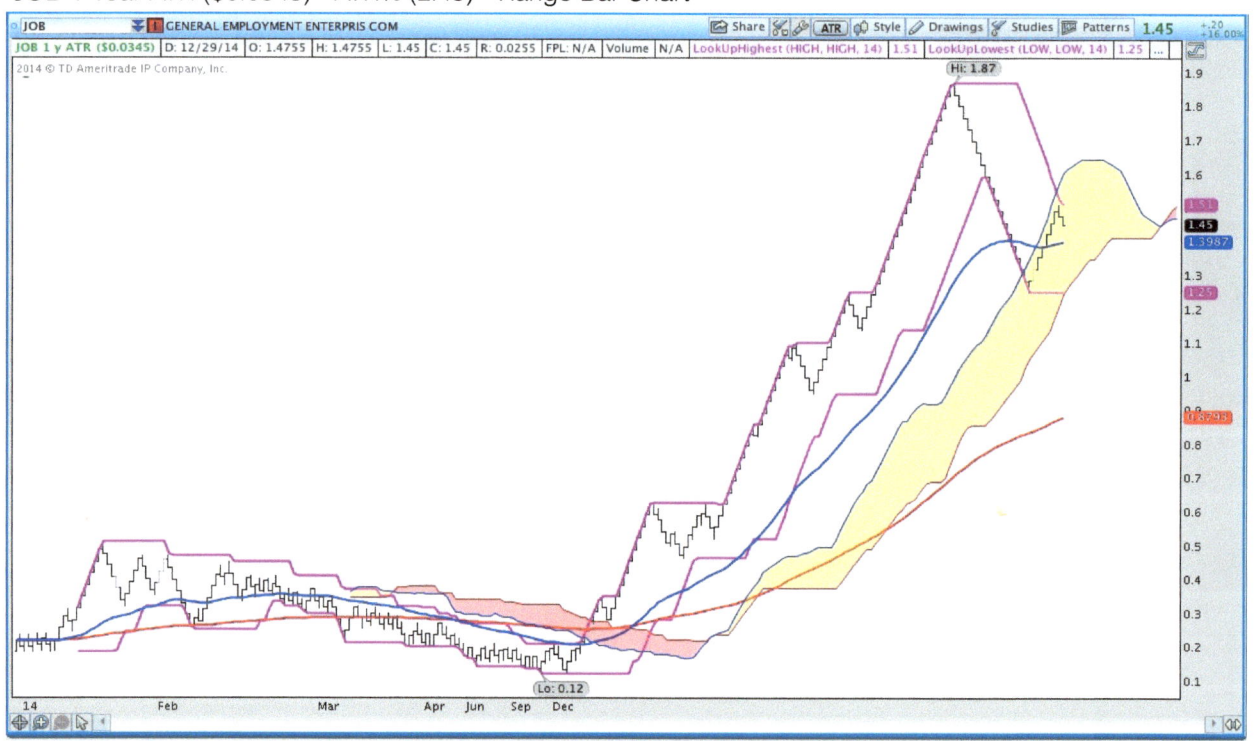

The previous (JOB Chart) is another example for the lag of the MA two lines Exceptional, while HH/LL confirmed the entry @ 0.21 and we took caution from Ichimoku Clouds resistance and preferred to wait until the price move over the cloud @ 0.27, the MA two lines Exceptional produced a buy signal (Golden cross) @ 0.55 which is double the late entry price from Ichimoku.

On the reverse, while HH/LL and Ichimoku Clouds produced sell signals around @1.60 to exit long position, MA two line Exceptional lagged and did not cross. If we were following it, we would lose at least 50% of the profits.

LIVE 1 Year ATR ($0.50) - ATR% (12.65) - Range Bar Chart

The previous (LIVE chart) saying it loudly "case closed | Rest in peace my dear MA wherever you are".

See the Golden cross around $2 in mid February and the Death cross happened around the same $2 in early May. If we were following it, we were to invest and spend 3 months for nothing.

While MA is the most widely used, it is not a reliable indicator to produce buying or selling signals.

Just like we said earlier, we can look at 50/200 MA two lines Exceptional only to confirm the interest of the crowd on any stock, not to take any action from our side regarding this stock either (Buy or Sell), since the crowd volume will not support any stock unless it have a Polish MA two lines.

RSI "Relative Strength Index" is the key player for entry

You know the old saying, keep the best for the last, this is true with RSI, we did focus from the beginning on price action because most of the indicators seem to be not effective, and truly lagging ones, but here is one leading indicator that was in test all the time and through my 10 years of experience, and made the highest percent when it comes to back-testing from professionals, it did made up to 73% winning ratio.

Ladies and gentlemen, let me introduce you the old RSI with our adjustment that proves to be the right one.

Developed by J. Welles Wilder, the Relative Strength Index (RSI) is a momentum oscillator that measures the speed and the change of price movements.

RSI oscillates between zero and 100.

Traditionally, and according to Wilder, RSI is considered overbought when above 70 and oversold when below 30.

Signals can also be generated by looking for divergences, failure swings and centerline crossovers.

RSI can also be used to identify the general trend.

RSI is an extremely popular momentum indicator that has been featured in a number of articles, interviews and books over the years.

Calculation

RSI = 100 - $\dfrac{100}{1 + RS}$

RS = Average Gain / Average Loss

To simplify the calculation explanation, RSI has been broken down into its basic components:

RS, Average Gain and Average Loss.

This RSI calculation is based on 14 periods, which is the default suggested by Wilder in his book.

Losses are expressed as positive values, not negative values.

The very first calculations for average gain and average loss are simple 14 period averages.

- First Average Gain = Sum of Gains over the past 14 periods / 14.

- First Average Loss = Sum of Losses over the past 14 periods / 14

The second, and subsequent, calculations are based on the prior averages and the current gain loss:

- Average Gain = [(previous Average Gain) x 13 + current Gain] / 14.

- Average Loss = [(previous Average Loss) x 13 + current Loss] / 14.

This is the normal set up for J. Welles Wilder, in our book we will adjust the bars calculated to 7 instead of 14, we will show you that unlike most of the professionals teaching us that over 70 territory is overbought, we do believe that we cannot enter into any trade unless its RSI hit 70 since any readings or trading before RSI hits 70 or what so called "Overbought Territory" is considered sideways and wasting of time and could cause us a big time loss.

Now, just like we said at the head of this chapter, RSI is the only key player in the right entry if we do not want to lose time and money.

Let's take a look at the next charts and see the reason behind it.

SPX 1 Year ATR ($17.17) - ATR% (0.82) - Range Bar Chart

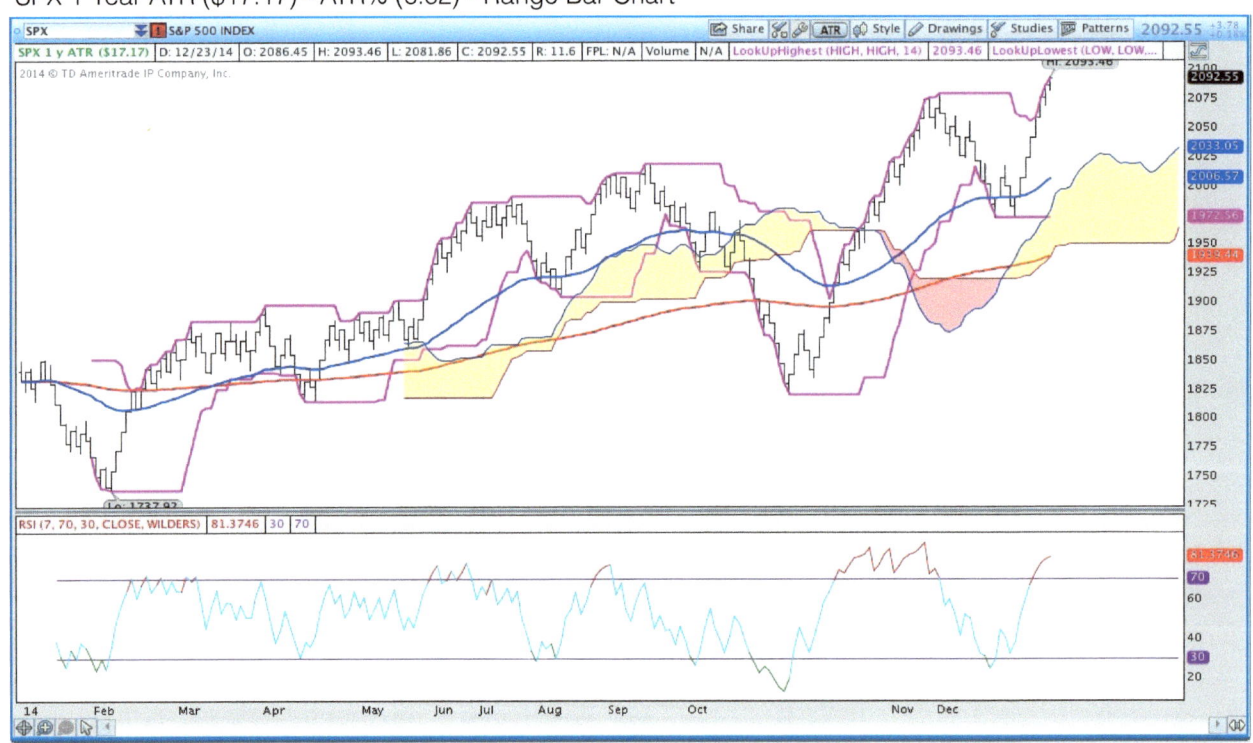

From the first glance, let's take a deep look at the price action itself from mid October till the beginning of December when the RSI 7 periods went to 70 level (overbought territory), check what happens to the price action, it did accelerated, right!!

You are right, one more advantage of using the Range Bar Charts that you can measure the indicators much better than any time-based charts, while monitoring hundreds of different stocks we did found that riding the trend in its beginning will be more accurate if the RSI were adjusted to 7 periods instead of 14 periods which is very late.

The other thing, RSI 7 Periods are matching identically with any true breakout when using the HH/LL study, also it is followed by a prove from Ichimoku Clouds.

As you can see in this chart the price hit the HH and penetrate its line and at the same time, RSI turns to red by crossing the "overbought territory" and start to accelerate.

Lets see another example that proves our saying.

JOB 1 Year ATR ($0.0345) - ATR% (2.43) - Range Bar Chart

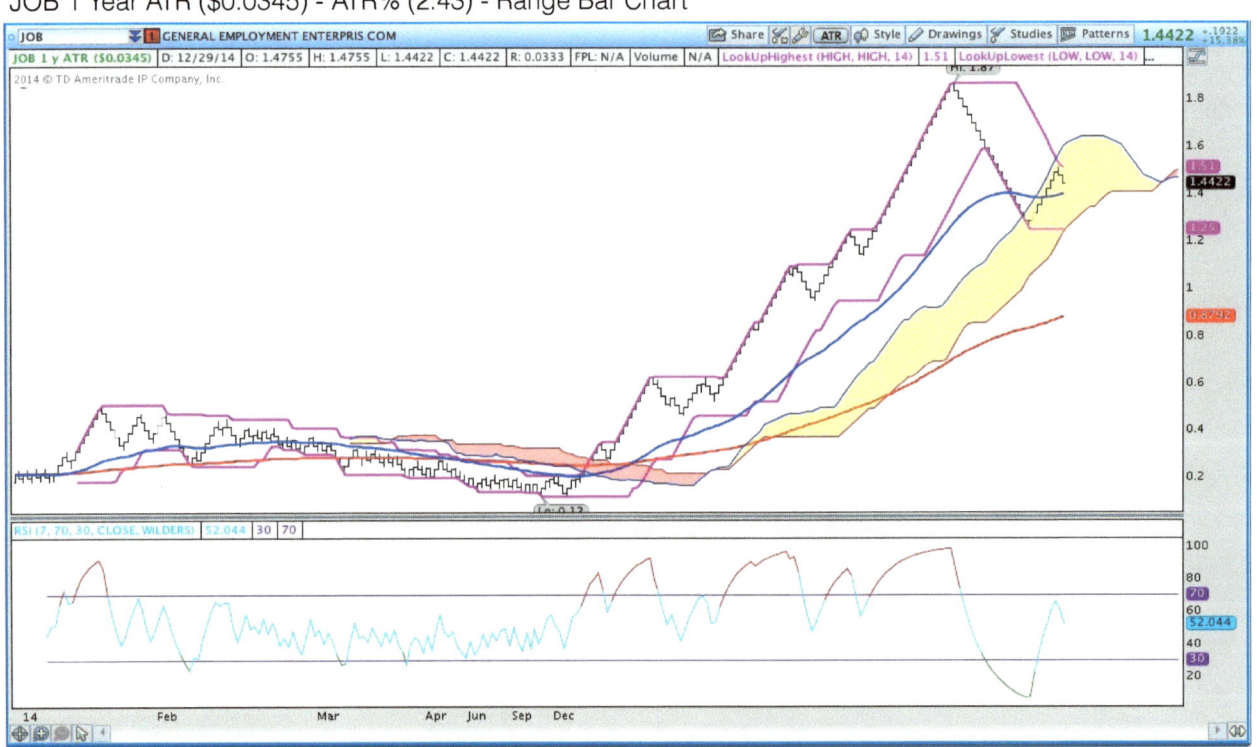

The previous (Job chart) is another example of what happens when RSI 7 periods did hit 70 level "Overbought territory", price action hit the highest high @ 0.21, at the same time and penetrate the line, and the rally starts all the way up to 1.87.

So kindly tell me which is wiser for swing and short term traders, to buy when we have two confirmations from RSI when it is in "overbought" state, followed by HighestHigh's line penetration!!!?, Or buy earlier than this and stuck in any stock for an unknown period of time playing the risky sideways.

Mentioning the volume issue, check me back at any time-based charts, and you will notice how huge the volume increased in the days of "overbought" state form RSI.

Let's look for a third example, and learn from it in the next chart.

LIVE 1 Year ATR ($0.50) - ATR% (12.65) - Range Bar Chart

In the same (LIVE chart) but in the previous chapter about HighestHigh - LowestLow, remember that we said that price action signaled a breakout and that the train is about to leave the station in a day or two, we just need to wait for a confirmation ticket from Ichimoku.

It is true but not enough because without confirmation from RSI when crossing 70 "Overbought territory", we have nothing, and it is useless and might be a false/ fake breakout.

Now the reading of RSI 7 Periods is around 64, so we **must wait** until it passes the 70 level readings, then and only then we have all confirmations in order, HighestHigh breakout, the blue line of Span A crossed over the red line of Span B and price crossed over the resistance cloud.

If this happens then we have a major up-trend, a strong rally that will maximize our chances, reduce our risk and save our time.

The final two words "Position-Sizing" and the winner is … YOU

POSITION-SIZING is an essential but often overlooked prerequisite to successful active trading.

After all, a trader who has generated substantial profits over his or her lifetime can lose it all in just one or two bad trades if proper position-sizing isn't employed.

Successful traders commonly quote the phrase: "Plan the trade and trade the plan." Just like in war, planning ahead can often mean the difference between success and failure.

Position-sizing is the part of your trading system that tells you "how much."

Once a trader has established the discipline to keep their stop loss on every trade, without question the most important area of trading is position-sizing.

Most people in mainstream Wall Street totally ignore this concept, but Van Tharp believes that position-sizing and psychology count for more than 90% of total performance (or 100% if every aspect of trading is deemed to be psychological).

Position-Sizing is the part of your trading system that tells you how many shares to take per trade.

Poor position-sizing is the reason behind almost every instance of account blowouts.

Preservation of capital is the most important concept for those who want to stay in the trading game for the long haul.

To determine you stock position-size, the steps and calculations are straightforward.

We will go through the steps and show some examples to help explain the process.

1.   First, decide how many stocks you want to keep in your portfolio.

Assume you have a portfolio of $50,000.

Assume that five is a reasonable number of stocks to properly track in your portfolio, you should only invest approximately $10,000 in each stock ($50,000 / 5 = $10,000).

2.   Second, establish how much you are willing to lose on a trade.

To get a good night's sleep I am willing to risk 5% on a trade.

This gives me the amount I am willing to lose.

Taking 5% of the $10,000 for each stock gives you $500 you are willing to lose on this trade.

3.   Third, establish your stop. As mentioned stops can be set at a specific price based on your reading of the chart, lets say right behind the LowestLow line.

You have set the stop for XYZ Corporation at $13.5.

4.   Determine your buy price.

Using our method to decide on your purchase price.

In this example, we are buying XYZ Corporation at 15.

5.   Fifth, calculate the size of the position. First the formula for those that are interested.

Position size = ((portfolio size / # of stocks to be held) * (amount willing to risk)) / (buy price – stop price)

Position size for XYZ Corp. = (($50,000 / 5) = $10,000 per position; ($10,000 * 5%)) / (15 – 13.5) = 333 shares to be bought.

By now, you notice that you are only spending $5,000 to buy 333 shares of XYZ Corporation at 15.

That is half of the risk capital you were willing to commit for your stock purchase.

This is telling you, you are more risk averse. Probably a good thing.

The reason for the discrepancy has to do with the variables that go into the calculation.

First, you are willing to risk a set percent.

Changes in the percent to risk will change the amount you are willing to risk.

Next, the stop price will affect the amount you are willing to risk.

Notice a theme. Each variable helps to establish how much you are willing to risk. This is the power of dynamically calculating the size of your position.

What if you were willing to risk 10%!!?.

Position-sizing is an excellent way to help add trading discipline to your investing decisions.

There are several position-sizing calculators available on the Internet.

The one described here follows the dynamically calculated approach as it allows you to change several factors to establish the best position-size for your portfolio.

And the winner is … *YOU*